To my mother, Gerri, for her endless love

JANETTA OTTER-BARRY BOOKS

Eye on the Wild: Brown Bear copyright © Frances Lincoln Limited 2012
Text and photographs copyright © Suzi Eszterhas 2012

The right of Suzi Eszterhas to be identified as the author and photographer of this work
has been asserted by her in accordance with the Copyright, Designs and Patents Act,
1988 (United Kingdom).]

First published in Great Britain and in the USA in 2012 by
Frances Lincoln Children's Books, 4 Torriano Mews,
Torriano Avenue, London NW5 2RZ
www.franceslincoln.com

A catalogue record for this book is available from the British Library.

ISBN 978-1-84780-302-3

Set in Stempel Schneidler

Printed in Dongguan, Guangdong, China by Toppan Leefung in March, 2012

1 3 5 7 9 8 6 4 2

BROWN BEAR

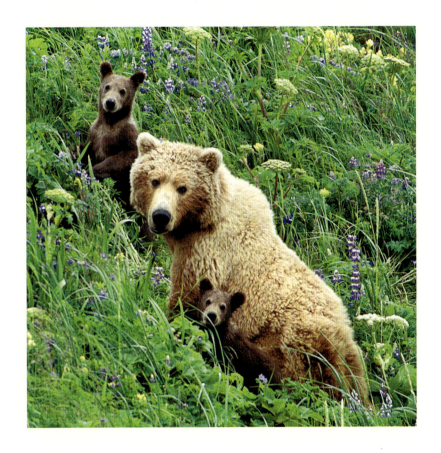

Suzi Eszterhas

F

FRANCES LINCOLN
CHILDREN'S BOOKS

Far away in the mountains of Alaska, in the middle of winter, two baby brown bears are born. It is so cold outside that they spend the first few months of their lives tucked away in a warm and cozy den, fast asleep next to Mom. They don't venture into the outside world until spring arrives, and the weather is getting warmer. When they do eventually leave their den, Mom stays close beside them.

The baby bears are called 'cubs' and look a lot like teddy bears. Even though they are five months old when they leave the den, they are still very small and need their mom's constant love and attention. They will stay right by her side for the next two years.

The cubs love their mom's milk so much that, when they are drinking, they hum to themselves contentedly. They are rather like happy cats purring. Mom will keep feeding them lots of milk until they are almost as big as she is.

Mom takes her babies everywhere she goes and they have many exciting adventures. They cross rivers, explore fields of flowers, laze around in grass meadows, and even go to the beach to play in the sand. But Mom is always watching over them to make sure they stay safe and don't get into trouble.

While the family is out exploring, the two young bears eat a lot of fresh, green grass. The grass is crunchy and tastes deliciously sweet. It is a very healthy food and helps to wake up their tummies after their long, winter sleep.

The young cubs are bursting with energy. They love to play-fight, chase each other, and climb about on logs. The games they play are great fun, but they also help the bears to grow big and strong, and they teach them essential survival skills that will be important when they have to survive on their own.

After all their adventures, it's time for a nap. Mom guards her cubs while they are fast asleep – always on the look-out for danger. A brown bear mom is one of the bravest moms on Earth, and she will do anything to protect her babies.

When autumn arrives, it's time to go fishing. Mom is an expert! When she spots a tasty-looking salmon in the river, she charges into the water at top speed and makes a huge splash. She uses her long claws as hooks to catch the fish when it tries to swim away.

A brown bear likes nothing more than a tasty salmon to eat – and the two cubs love the taste of it right away. So Mom is kept busy catching enough fish to feed herself and her two hungry offspring. The rich oil in the fish will give the family the fat they need to stay warm throughout the freezing, cold winter to come.

But brown bears don't eat only salmon. They eat lots of different foods. They even love to eat clams and, on warm summer days, Mom takes her youngsters to the beach to find these sweet treats. Looking for clams is like a treasure hunt and the cubs use their paws to turn over rocks and dig deep in the sand.

The cubs are growing bigger and braver every day and, after nearly two years, they are almost as big as Mom. But they are still young and have a great deal more to learn before she lets them out into the wide world on their own.

As the cubs grow older, Mom teaches them to fish for their own salmon and they spend day after day in the river. Fishing lessons aren't as much fun as playing, but the cubs need to learn how to find the best fishing spots and the different ways to catch their prey.

Catching fish is not easy! At first, the cubs splash about too much and scare the fish away. Or they jump and miss, so a lot of fish manage to escape. But eventually the cubs get really good at fishing – almost as good as Mom.

When the cubs are two-and-a-half years old, Mom's work is finally done. She has taught them how to fish, how to find clams and other food, how to make a winter den, and how to stay out of danger. Now Mom has to leave them. But the two cubs will stay together for a while longer.

The two young bears
still like to play-fight just
like when they were babies.
They are careful not to
hurt each other and use
their huge paws like boxing
gloves. This helps them
to learn how to protect
themselves now that
Mom has gone.

The young bears celebrate their third birthday together, hidden away in a warm winter den, where they spend as long as five months fast asleep. At last, spring arrives and it's warm enough to venture outside. They leave the den and say goodbye to each other. Now they are ready for their biggest adventure yet – starting families of their own.

More about Brown Bears

- Brown bears live in North America, Europe and Asia.

- Brown bears are the second-largest bears in the world, after polar bears. Male brown bears can weigh over 1,000 pounds and stand nearly 10 feet tall.

- Brown bears are not always brown. Their thick fur may be black, cinnamon, auburn, or even blond.

- Brown bears will eat almost anything. Most of their diet is fish, berries, herbs, roots, nuts, flowers, grasses, and other vegetation. But they also eat insects, honey, small mammals, and even elk.

- Brown bears have very good noses and can smell things from nearly a mile away.

- In early fall, when brown bears are feeding on salmon, they can gain up to 30 pounds a day. They will live off this fat during their long winter hibernation.

- During hibernation, a bear's body functions slow down, and its heartbeat drops from 40–70 beats a minute to about 8–12 beats a minute.

- Brown bears are endangered because people are hunting them and destroying their home.

- For more information visit www.raincoast.org